**What peopl.          ___,...g about *LEAPFROG*:**

*Janet Givens has captured the essence of civil conversation in the clever acronym LEAPFROG. In restorative justice work, we begin with establishing that there is something in this universe which connects us. It might be where we live, it might be our ancestry; often it is our shared values that help us move a conversation from trying to convince to being curious. Thank you, Janet, for paving the way. May we all be courageous enough to initiate a civil conversation.* Susan Cherry, Executive Director, The Community Restorative Justice Center, Inc., St. Johnsbury, Vermont

*Janet's LEAPFROG describes— in an accessible and fun way— the nuts and bolts of how to have a civil conversation and how to effectively remain neutral in the context of an encounter with someone with a different view. This is a tool to use every day!* Karen Bufka, community organizer, St. Johnsbury, Vermont

Also by Janet Givens

*Stuttering* (part of the Pro-Ed series on
communication disorders; with C. W. Starkweather)

*At Home on the Kazakh Steppe: A Peace Corps Memoir*

# LEAPFROG:

*How to hold a civil conversation in an uncivil era*

Janet Givens, M.A.

Birch Tree Books, Danville, Vermont

Also available as an eBook.

*LEAPFROG: How to hold a civil conversation in an uncivil era*

Text © Janet Givens 2019
Cover design © Anne McKinsey 2019
Cover image by naobim from Pixabay


Published by Birch Tree Books, 2019

Also available as an eBook.

## DEDICATED

to my grandchildren:

Mikah, Elijah, Isabella, Raleigh, and Kendall

It's time for us adults to stop wishing for peace and start working for it. I hope this booklet helps.

*Talking about "those people" instead of
talking with each other is a poor excuse for
genuine political discourse.*
Parker Palmer, <u>Healing the Heart of Democracy</u>

# TABLE OF CONTENTS

# ACKNOWLEDGEMENTS

Karen Bufka, working to get a League of Women Voters chapter established in St. Johnsbury, asked me to present to the group on civil discourse. This started the LEAPFROG ball rolling and I am most grateful to her.

Shanna Ratner is State Coordinator for Better Angels, St. Albans, Vermont and was the moderator of a Better Angels Skills Workshop I attended in April, 2019. Her feedback helped me keep this a bi-partisan handbook and I thank her.

For over thirty years, my friend Jeanne Shea has been offering her razor-sharp eye and insightful understanding to my writing since she typed my first research paper during my grad school days. We don't always agree, but I am grateful for her friendship as well as her integrity and good eye.

The readers of my blog, *And So It Goes*, read the original chapters and were generous and supportive in their comments. One of those readers, Sharon Lippincott, sent an unexpected contribution at a precipitous time. Her support convinced me a book was a possibility. I am grateful to them all.

Rima Shaeffer, Lindsay de Feliz, Susan Taylor, Kim Crady-Smith, Robyn Greenstone, Barb Armstrong, Martha Hill, Robyn Morrison, and the members of my End of the Road Writers' Group led by Reeve Lindberg were generous with their time and their feedback; each one helped make the book better and I appreciate their support.

My thanks also go to three professionals who first helped me with my *At Home* memoir and were there for me again with *LEAPFROG*: Anne McKinsey of AMCK Web and Print designed the cover; Kelly Boyer Sagert, gave the book a needed final editing, and Maria Novillo Saravia of BeauteBook formatted the paperback. To each of them I say an appreciative Thank You.

Finally, my husband, Woody Starkweather, is always ready with his discerning eye to read my work and never says "no" to me. For that I am truly blessed.

# INTRODUCTION

**Why am I writing this book?** My government, this unique American democracy, has long been an exciting experiment to me. Constantly striving to improve, her watchwords, until recently, have been progress and inclusion.

She has made many tragic mistakes over her nearly 250 years. The depravity of slavery, the genocide of our Native population, the blatant discrimination of each succeeding wave of immigrants, and the arrogance of interning Americans of Japanese descent during WWII are only the most well-known. America's history is filled with examples of the kind of "dehumanization" at the core of our current incivility.

And yet, we have grown from those mistakes. We've changed the laws and we've gotten stronger as waves of immigrants brought new blood and new ideas onto our land. This diversity is one of our greatest strengths as a country and, for many, defines who we are as Americans.

Some would say that is a liberal point of view and, wanting to be certain this booklet attracts all Americans, I turned to the cognitive linguist George Lakoff for guidance. Lakoff has written (in *Moral Politics: How Liberals and Conservatives Think*) of American voters as falling into two distinct metaphors of family structure: the strict, authoritarian parent (conservatives) and the nurturing parent (liberals).

According to Lakoff, discipline, obedience, and patriotism align strongly with conservative worldviews. As a result, the issues of military might, national security, and crime will be viewed differently by conservatives and liberals. Even "responsibility" gets divided, with conservatives advocating for personal responsibility and liberals, social responsibility.

Liberals push for multiculturalism and advocate for travel and new experiences (it was the Democratic presidency of John F. Kennedy that gave us the Peace Corps, for example), while conservative values of tradition, stability, and an affinity for the familiar have also woven themselves throughout our history and have helped to steady the ship of state during times of upheaval. Indeed, the mixture of conservative and liberal positions is yet one more example of the range of American diversity.

This diversity is now at risk, as is the stability we once took for granted. My concern around the unprecedented (in my lifetime) level of incivility we are currently experiencing is that we face critical challenges as we look ahead. We can all come up with our own critical challenges list, I'm sure. The point is, whatever the challenge we face, we must learn to talk to those with whom we disagree. The alternative is wholly unacceptable.

Keep in mind, we are talking about our brothers and sisters, our uncles and aunts, our fellow citizens; people in relationships that matter to us who hold strong opinions, have needs they want met, and vote.

Gaps among our various demographic groups widen with each new poll. But I believe we can come together as a country, we can meet the challenges ahead if we can only learn talk to one another. If we don't start today, then when? If not you, then who?

**When did we stop talking to each other?** When I was growing up, the Emily Post books on etiquette taught that, in polite conversation, we must stay away from politics and religion, two topics that are central to how we see ourselves. And, back when we would have had guests of divergent belief systems, we'd opt for dinner party civility over winning an argument.

But these days we don't have to stay away from those topics because we hang out more and more with those who think and live and vote and worship as we do. Ideological bubbles, we call them, and we all live comfortably within their familiar borders.

Worse, as more schools eliminate classes in civics and cancel debate teams, critical thinking and rhetoric skills suffer. Rhetoric teaches us to argue without anger; debate offers the chance to argue a position dispassionately by taking one opposite your own. Wouldn't they be valuable skills to foster?

Our country is struggling today with countless issues — "God, guns, and gays" someone once alliterated. Going deeper, these issues are often about who gets to decide who holds the power, and how porous the boundary is that separates the "Haves" from the "Have-nots."

In a pure monarchy, royalty rules. In a democracy, it's the people, and merit is what counts. In an oligarchy, the wealthy decide based upon how they might increase their wealth, while the rest of the citizenry are kept at bay by pitting the people against each other. Is that where we are today?

The need for people of diverse views to be able to talk

together has a history as long as democracy itself – back to the Greeks. Socrates taught that civil discourse was a "dialectic" — a public dialogue to uncover truth — and would resolve conflicts within a society. Later, Cicero, the Roman orator and statesman of the first century BC, introduced the term civil society (*societas civilis*) and held that human beings are inherently rational and have the capacity to gather for a common cause to maintain peace. That era ended when feudalism arrived and the idea of "Just War" preoccupied political thought until the Enlightenment of the 18th century, theoretically at least.

After spending the last two years researching and collecting stories, I'm more convinced than ever that we all benefit from ideas that challenge us and get us to think anew. No matter our political, religious, or philosophical beliefs, we can disagree without becoming disagreeable. More importantly, we can disagree with someone we love and still love them.

In our current political climate, our cultural capacity for sustained discussion over serious disagreement is low. Anyone watching news shows where guests are reduced to shouting over each other can attest to this loss of civility.

**Conflict, disagreement, and misunderstanding can arise unexpectedly during the course of anyone's day.**

And, while remaining civil is not always easy, it is important to remember that hate and fear are neither the natural nor necessary responses to difference. Nevertheless, we may get triggered, sucked into an argument we didn't see coming, propping one set of facts up against another with neither side listening, and eventually wondering what the hell just happened. We say more about this moment in Chapters 3 (Assess) and 7 (Observe).

As important as political conversations are, the ideas given here can be applied to any conversation you deem "difficult," from marital disagreements and parent-teen clashes to neighborhood standoffs and workplace disputes. And so, perhaps a more inclusive subtitle would be, *How to Hold a Difficult Conversation at a Difficult Time.*

In any case, the first goal of these conversations is understanding. A difficult conversation need not diminish the other person's self-worth, question the other's judgment, engage in name calling, threats, or bullying. And, of equal importance, these conversations are not intended to convert or convince.

Not intended, that's the important point. One or the other of you may wind up changing your point of view. This is not to be negated, of course. But, it is important to understand the steps outlined in this booklet will not work if you set out thinking one of you just needs to change.

Instead, think of your disagreement as a mystery that intrigues you both. Strive together to discover just where your impasse is, why it is you disagree so vigorously. What have each of you not understood until now? If you can think of it as an adventure you're undertaking together, and you'll go far.

> *Civility does not mean the mere outward gentleness of speech cultivated for the occasion, but an inborn gentleness and desire to do the opponent good.*
> Mahatma Gandhi

**LEAPFROG, an acronym comprised of four verbs and four nouns,** grew from my notes on civil discourse that I presented to my local League of Women Voters group in early 2017. Those notes became a series of ten blog posts, which my readers convinced me should be gathered into a book. Here we are, two years later.

The verbs are **L**isten, **E**mpathize, **A**ssess, and **P**araphrase. Together, they help us as we listen to the other person. The four nouns — **F**acts (Forget them for now), **R**espect, **O**bservation, and **G**ratitude — guide us as we present our ideas in a way that will increase the likelihood that we will also be heard. Yes, it's all about listening and being heard.

I present these eight elements linearly only to form an easily remembered acronym. Feel free to leap, jump, or bounce around, taking turns and repeating the elements as your conversation continues, leapfrog fashion, back and forth, taking you deeper into understanding, appreciation, and, ideally, connection.

**At the end of each chapter,** I'll present questions for you to consider. I hope you'll take the time to reflect on them before you move on.

For this introduction, I want to honor the fact that there are cultural as well as individual differences in how we deal with conflict. To that end, please consider these questions before proceeding:

- What were the norms about conflict in your childhood home? How were disagreements managed? How did your family get their news? How were current events discussed?
- How have those early rules changed as you've matured? Are any subjects "off the table" automatically? How must someone behave for you to engage with them in a debate? How do you talk about current events with people who disagree with you?

I also hope you'll take advantage of the resources I've collected as I put this booklet together. You'll find them at the end of each chapter plus a broader list at the end of the book. The links are live in the eBook version and on the LEARN MORE page of my website, *janetgivens.com*

## Resources used in putting my initial **LEAPFROG** acronym together:

*Teaching Tolerance: A Project of the Southern Poverty Law Center*, more specifically their blog post, *Toward a More Civil Discourse*, April 2016.

National Institute for Civil Discourse at the University of Arizona

The Scheinman Institute on Conflict Resolution at Cornell University

Holly Weeks. *Failure to Communicate: How Conversations Go Wrong and What You Can Do to Right Them.* Harvard Business Review Press. 2010

NOTES

NOTES

# 1

## L is for Listen

If it is our desire to live in a civil society, a good society, we must be willing to engage in a dialogue with those with whom we disagree. This is the premise with which I begin. But how do we do that? Particularly when the likelihood is high that it will go awry?

Every difficult conversation begins with listening and good listening starts with curiosity. You might think of it as a mystery the two of you are hoping to solve together. Are you interested in understanding the other person's position better? Are you curious what you'll learn?

What is both difficult and critical is to refrain from offering solutions or making judgments. How tempting it can be to jump to conclusions such as, *"They don't know what they're talking about."* Or *"Their facts are wrong."* Or, *"How ignorant they are."*

If you catch yourself doing this, that's OK. It's quite human. Just stop, regain your curiosity, and remember the mystery you hope to solve. Here are a few suggested openings for you.

*I'm curious about [your experience] and have been hoping to find someone I might talk with about it.*

*Would you be willing to have a conversation with me about our different view? Do you have any curiosity about [my experience]?*

*My goal is not to criticize. I am really just curious and wonder if you are too.*

*I've got this little booklet called LEAPFROG that says it can help us. Shall we have a go?*

Beyond being truly curious to understand what they believe, good listening also requires you to pay attention. This involves clarifying and acknowledging what you are hearing.

We ask questions to clarify our understanding of what has already been said.

*Did you say there were three reasons? I've got the first two; what was that third one?*

*I'm not sure I heard that last part. Can you repeat it, please?*

And we acknowledge as much as we can, understanding that acknowledging is not the same as agreeing.

*This sounds really important to you.*

The Greater Good Science Center in Berkeley, California tells us that practicing active listening can increase empathy and improve relationship satisfaction. And empathy is where we are going next.

**Here is a question to consider before moving on:**

- What challenges do you see in simply listening as a first step in a difficult conversation?

## A Resource for Chapter 1

**The Greater Good of Berkeley, CA offers a step-by-step summary of active listening from their page, Greater Good in Action's Active listening.**

# NOTES

## 2

## E is for Empathize

Empathy is an emotional investment we make, a choice to be present with the other person's experience. It involves paying attention to their body language and facial expressions, not just their words.

Listening with empathy expands our curiosity beyond the other person's beliefs to include what they are feeling: their sensations and emotions. And, it does so without judgment or defensiveness.

How often do we get the opportunity to be listened to, fully, compassionately, without interruption, and without the cost of a therapist? I think this type of listening is a gift we can give the other person. And vice versa.

Think of empathy as a muscle. While we are all born with the capacity to feel empathy, we must exercise it if it is to become truly useful. Here are a few suggestions for increasing our capacity for empathy in general:

- Read more fiction or see more plays. This helps us step outside of our own lives for a time.
- Pay attention to faces. This helps us practice having an interest in the other's emotional state. I practice this by nodding hello to strangers in grocery lines or elsewhere. Simply acknowledging the presence of other people is powerful and is a strong part of many cultures.
- Share in other people's joy. Empathy is not limited to commiserating; it can also be a response to emotions like happiness and pride.

It's not easy to empathize when we are feeling the myriad forms of anger, sadness, or fear. So, to that initial curiosity, we add compassion. "Born out of feeling the rawness of the heart," psychologist and author John Welwood has said, "compassion makes us more sensitive to others."

One way to enhance our compassion for the other person is to look for and find shared experiences and identities. You have identified your differences; that's why you are talking. See if you can identify the commonalities you share. Are you both grandparents? Recently married or widowed? Are you animal lovers?

Knowing what you hold in common might temper the tone as you move along. Here are some questions to help you identify commonalities:

*What activities do you find most fulfilling?*

*How can you/will you best contribute to the world?*

*What do you want your legacy to be?*

*What have been your greatest moments of happiness?*

*What talents and capacities do you have or want to have?*

*What are the things you would like to have? (e.g., a boat, an IRA, kids)*

*What kind of person do you aspire to be? (e.g., funny, kind, hardworking, smart)*

*What activities do you aspire to do? (Do you want to travel, get a degree, own your own business?)*

## Questions for you to ponder before moving on:

- Can you identify one person with whom you might practice having a difficult conversation and schedule a time to sit together? What might keep you from doing such a thing?

## Resources for Chapter 2

Wonder how empathetic you are? See the 28-question quiz put out by The Greater Good of Berkeley, CA that pulls from three separate research studies on empathy.

Roman Krznaric, Australian political sociologist, offers an "Empathy Library" for stretching that empathy muscle. He also has a YouTube video talking about **empathy** as a force for social change, how it can create a revolution in human relationships, and how it is at the core of any social movement.

Paul Parkin's TEDx video, *Reimagining Empathy: The Transformative Nature of Empathy* tells us that when we cultivate empathy, we enlarge our capacity to receive empathy.

And, for a slightly different take on empathy, see my blog post on *The Downside of Empathy*, April 2018.

# NOTES

**3**

## A is for Assess

Assess, as I'm using it here, simply means to ask yourself, "Is this a conversation I am able to have at this time?" This is more important than you may initially realize.

Having our core belief system challenged is frightening. Once our amygdala kicks in (as a primitive response to threat), we are functioning in default mode and are less likely to be curious enough to participate effectively in a difficult conversation. Continuing will not only serve no useful purpose, it may even backfire (as we'll discuss in Chapter 5: F).

You need not engage with anyone filled with contempt or threatening violence. Likewise, racism, sexism, misogyny, xenophobia, homophobia, Islamophobia — any of these active prejudicial biases — will sabotage a civil conversation. Remember, while LEAPFROG can guide you through particularly difficult conversations, you need to determine if this is the conversation you sought, one grounded in curiosity and compassion on both sides.

Difficult conversations, by definition, expose the choices we make and the values that inform those choices. Such exposure may leave us feeling vulnerable. When we begin, not knowing where these conversations will lead, we step into a mysterious unknown. And yes, that can be scary.

Think of your willingness to assess the conversation as a form of self-care. Here are three steps to help.

### 1. Pause

At any part of the conversation, know you can take a moment and reassess. If your pause becomes conspicuous, simply name it.

*Hold on just a moment. I need to check in with myself.*

And, if you want to leave the room, try this:

*I need a bit of time before I continue. I'll return in _____ minutes.*

In either case, take a few slow belly breaths and remember that silence can be your friend. We'll say more about belly breaths in Chapter 7 (Observation).

## 2. Think

**Think about the person with whom you are talking.**

Who are they in their everyday life? Can you see them also as a parent, neighbor, friend, relative, someone's child?

From your work in Chapter 2 (Empathy), do you know what goals they have? Do they seek respect, attention, power, acknowledgment, control, independence, security? Which goals do you share?

Have you identified values you share? You might explore your beliefs about achievement, status, recognition, power, money, family, health, adventure, risk, change, serenity, security, self-reliance, freedom, liberty, love, faith. Can you think of others?

Do the commonalities you share help you feel more connected or not?

Keep in mind that most people operate out of habit and none of us can change if we don't know any other way.

**Think about yourself.**

How **curious** are you?

Are you aware of the assumptions you hold? Assumptions

can become self-fulfilling prophecies. For example, if you enter the conversation assuming, "This is going to be a battle," chances are, it will be.

What are your own needs and fears? Do you feel unequal to the other person in some way? Whether you feel superior, better educated, or intimidated, pay attention. Are you aware of the inherent biases you hold?

Why are you really engaging in the conversation? Be aware if it is still to understand, or if it is to change the other.

Have you found compassion for your conversation partner? Good. Now have some for yourself as you recognize the courage it takes to hold this conversation.

### 3. Name Your Truth

The ability to name what is true for you — including an unexpected assumption or an unexamined bias — is powerful. You can choose to state these out loud or simply acknowledge them to yourself for now.

Here are a few suggestions for when you are ready to state your truth. And, really, what have you got to lose by putting out there what is true for you?

*I'm feeling uncomfortable at the direction this conversation is going.*

*I'm starting to feel defensive here; that's not going to help.*

*I'm feeling angry at what you just said. Give me a minute to figure out what I need to do.*

You might also discover some positive reactions on your part. Acknowledge them too.

*I like how you said that. Now I can understand where you're coming from a bit better.*

*I'm enjoying how this is going.*

For too many, a possibly useful conversation stops with the recognition that the opposing point of view feels threatening. Please remember that the majority of the work in any conflict is with yourself. It's a powerful feeling to be able to check in with yourself effectively. Be as specific as possible and know that this is easier for some than others.

Keep in mind that if you can share your truth aloud, no matter what it may be, you may very well enable the conversation to go deeper. We will return to this idea in the FROG sections. For now, if you've decided this is the conversation for you and the time is right, it's time for our next chapter: P is for Paraphrase what you have heard.

**Something to consider first:**

Naming and sharing your feelings are new behaviors for many people. You might take some time to practice with a trusted friend, relative, or professional until it becomes more familiar to you.

## A Resource for Chapter 3

Without the training I received at the Pennsylvania Gestalt Center, I could not have written Chapter 3. For more information on that training and the woman at the forefront of it, please see my blog post on Mariah Fenton Gladis (August, 2018) and visit their website.

NOTES

# NOTES

# 4

# P is for Paraphrase

How can you be certain that what you've heard is what was meant? How do you know you understand? Simple enough to ask; not necessarily easy to achieve.

Start by summarizing what you think you've heard. If you get it wrong, simply ask them to clarify, then paraphrase again. Keep doing this until you receive some version of, "Yes, that's what I'm saying."

Realize though that it is not always easy for someone to hear their words rearranged, particularly if it is for the first time. So when you do summarize, do so with compassion. Remember, you are taking someone else's beliefs and condensing them; simplifying them, perhaps. Our beliefs are grounded in our values, consciously or not; so take care.

It's also possible that they have not really thought their position through. So, when they hear your words, the reality of their position may hit them for the first time. They may be pleasantly surprised. Or, they may be unpleasantly surprised.

Here are some ways you might begin:

*What I hear you saying is . . .*

*Do I understand you to mean . . . ?*

*You believe that . . . Is this correct?*

Ideally, your conversation partner will be willing to work with you to fine tune your summary until you are both clear that you have heard what was intended. Or, you may find instead a response that brings you back to Chapter 3, assessing whether this is the conversation for you to have at this time or not.

Keep in mind, as in any game of LEAPFROG, these steps happen over and over and over. You are both taking turns listening (actively and with empathy), assessing whether you want to continue in the discussion or not, and paraphrasing what you have heard in a way that assures you both that you understand accurately.

The elements in LEAP are designed to help when you are listening. The four elements we will cover in FROG are designed to help when you are speaking.

You'll find, I hope, that the more you repeat each step, the deeper and more meaningful will be your conversation and, as a result, the deeper and more meaningful will be your connection to each other.

**Before LEAPing into FROG, here are the questions to address first.**

- Are you dreading that annual family gathering because you know that you're the only one who voted the way you did and the subject is going to come up?
- Do neighborhood gatherings always end in a political argument?
- Do you secretly cringe when your seat mate on the commuter line you frequent, someone you've liked and who appeared so sensible, makes a blatantly political comment that shocks you?
- What is it about these situations that troubles you the most?

**A Resource for Chapter 4**

For those with little experience paraphrasing someone else's words, there's a comprehensive review of the important points to keep in mind. Written by Carter McNamara, it's on a professional coaching site called Management Help and is entitled *How to Paraphrase and Summarize.*

# NOTES

NOTES

# 5

## F is for Facts

### (forget them at first)

Contrary to popular opinion, the research is fairly clear that we choose our facts to support our beliefs and values, not the other way around. Even more troubling, facts, when introduced too soon, can backfire.

In the mid-2000s, two political scientists conducted four experiments in which subjects read mock news articles that included either a misleading claim from a politician, or a misleading claim and a correction. Not only did their results indicate that "corrections frequently fail to reduce misperceptions among the targeted ideological group," they also found several instances in which corrections actually increased misperceptions.

Political scientists Brendan Nyhan and Jason Reifler

dubbed this phenomenon "the backfire effect" and defined it this way: *Confronting a belief with facts to the contrary often strengthens the initial belief.*

Nyhan and Reifler make an important distinction between being uninformed and being misinformed. They are interested in the latter and find that it's the misinformed who often hold the strongest political beliefs. In a follow-up article in *The Boston Globe*, reporter Joe Keohane summarizes their findings:

> *In reality, we often base our opinions on our beliefs, which can have an uneasy relationship with facts. And rather than facts driving beliefs, our beliefs can dictate the facts we choose to accept. They can cause us to twist facts so they fit better with our preconceived notions. Worst of all, they can lead us to uncritically accept bad information just because it reinforces our beliefs. This reinforcement makes us more confident we're right, and even less likely to listen to any new information. And then we vote.*

You've no doubt heard of "confirmation bias," that very human tendency to choose facts that support our already firmly held opinions as we discount those that don't. It's one of many cognitive biases that befall those deeply attached to their beliefs. Googling "confirmation bias" or "cognitive biases" will bring you a plethora of further information. I'll let you sort through them

I also want to call your attention to the brain, specifically your amygdala and your hypothalamus.

Tucked inside the primitive part of our brain, our **amygdala** served us well eons ago when the now-extinct hairy mastodon was headed our way. But, this tiny sliver of our brain is not very good at discriminating a real from a perceived threat.

At the risk of badly oversimplifying, the fear we felt when the mastodon was at the mouth of our cave feels no different from the fear we feel today when we believe our sense of who we are, our identity, is threatened. When that identity is attached to a particular set of beliefs that have just been attacked, we click into survival mode. Or, as a fascinating new body of literature calls it, our amygdala has been hijacked.

Oxytocin, the trust hormone, flows when we feel safe and warm and fuzzy. Produced in our **hypothalamus** and secreted via our pituitary gland, oxytocin gives us a nice buzz. And, liking that buzz, we want more.

Safe, warm, and fuzzy happens when we:

- Stick with what's familiar (versus engaging in something

41

new, which can be scary),

- Know what's coming next (versus sitting in the unknown, which can be scary), and
- Hang with those who validate us: our tribe (versus being with someone who challenges us, which can be scary).

Are you seeing a pattern here? The new, the unknown, and the challenging can be scary.

Remember this when you find yourself sitting across the turkey from Uncle Bob who declares that "*XYZ is a charlatan and a crook and should be in jail.*" Or Aunt Betty complains about the strange family that just moved in down the street and how her "*property values will now plummet.*" Or Cousin Rudy announces plans to buy himself "*a brand new Uzi because it's my constitutional right.*" Perhaps you'll now better understand the intensity behind their views.

And remember, too, it's our attachment to being right that causes us so much trouble.

I grew up in the 20th century when the following aphorism was popular. Perhaps you'll recognize it.

*If people are ignorant, facts will enlighten them. If they are mistaken, facts will set them straight.*

It was not a new idea. In the mid-19th century, President Abraham Lincoln, said:

*I am a firm believer in the people. If given the truth, they can be depended upon to meet any national crisis. The great point is to bring them the real facts.*

Go back another seventy-five years and President Thomas Jefferson held a similar view:

*Whenever the people are well-informed, they can be trusted with their own government.*

Yes, it's a long-standing American belief. One that reinforces why our democracy provides for a free, public education through high school and secures for us a free press and the right to peacefully assemble. We want an informed, engaged citizenry.

Unfortunately, our two esteemed presidents notwithstanding, facts aren't necessarily going to help.

When someone's "truth" contradicts ours, how seductive to believe the other is "ignorant" or "mistaken." How tempting to think we can convert the other if we just choose the right words, use the right tone. Armed with our facts, we march into battle.

However, since understanding is our goal, we must ignore facts. For now. They have their place in any conversation, of course, but first, receptivity, a willingness to hear them, must exist. On both sides.

Toward that end, we can humanize our differing beliefs by sharing a story about the life experiences that led us to hold them. Telling our stories puts a human face and transports us all. They must come first, before the facts.

**Once you have used the LEAPFROG model for a few turns** (remember how the game is played), it might be time to present your facts. If so, the small *Debunking Handbook* by John Cook and Stephen Lewendowski is your go-to for effective strategies. (See the Resources List at the end of this chapter.)

To make it even easier, I've rearranged their ideas to form the acronym CAGE: **C**ore facts, **A**lternative explanation, **G**raphics, and **E**xplicit warnings as your cliff-notes version of how to present your facts.

1. **Core facts.** Focus on key facts in a refutation, not the myth.

2. **Alternative explanation.** Fill any gaps left by your

debunking with an alternative causal explanation (for why the myth is wrong and, optionally, why the misinformers promoted the myth in the first place).

**3. Graphics.** Present core facts graphically if possible. Visuals help.

**4. Explicit warnings.** Use visual or textual cues to warn the "other" before debunking the myth.

**Your question to ponder before moving on:**

• Think back to your last political conversation. Or, your last Town Hall meeting. Or, your last family feast that ended badly. Which part of CAGE was missing? What went wrong?

## Resources for Chapter 5

Janet Givens. *Blame it on the oxytocin ... with its magic spell.* 2016. *And So It Goes*, at *janetgivens.com*

John Cook and Stephen Lewendowski. *The Debunking Myth*. 2012. Available as a free PDF download.

Jason Reifler and Brendan Nyhan. "Opening the Political Mind? The effects of self affirmation and graphical information on factual misperceptions." 2011. Available at brendon-nyhan.com/blog

David Gal and Derek Rucker. "When in Doubt, Shout! — Paradoxical Influences of Doubt on Proselytizing." 2010. Available online at journals.sagepub.com

Joe Keohane. *The Boston Globe*, "How Facts Backfire. Researchers discover a surprising threat to democracy: our brains." 2010.

Brendan Nyhan and Jason Reifler. "When Corrections Fail: The persistence of political misperceptions." *Political Behavior 32(2)*: 303-330. 2010.

David Redlawsk. "Hot Cognition or Cool Consideration? Testing the Effects of Motivated Reasoning on Political Decision Making." 2003. Available at onlinelibrary.wiley.com

James Kuklinski. "Misinformation and the Currency of Democratic Citizenship." 2000.

Leon Festinger, Henry Riecken, and Stanley Schacter. *When Prophecy Fails*. Simon & Schuster. 1959.

# NOTES

NOTES

# 6

# R is for Respect

How easy it is to lump "those who have caused my distress" together as the "other" and blame them. "You made me . . ." points a finger and lets us abdicate responsibility for our discomfort by putting it on to the other. This dehumanization, this blame, this demonization forms the ground of incivility.

When we forget our common humanity, we create a chasm between us that is hard to bridge. Respect serves as a bridge to cross that chasm.

There is a spiritual dimension to respect that appeals to me. It requires us to step back, to understand the wider implications, to see the bigger picture, to take the "God view," and recognize how deeply we are connected to one another.

We all believe we are unbiased observers of our world. But bias is an equal opportunity influencer. All of us, at one time or another, have allowed our biases to color our perceptions, our attitudes, and yes, our beliefs. And we do this mostly unaware.

Respect requires us to let go of our need to be right and acknowledge that we all resist being wrong. Respect asks us to consider the possibility that we don't really know and to recognize the other's capacity to figure their life out. Simply, we acknowledge that the other's reality, though different from ours, is deserving of our respect.

My concern around the unprecedented level of incivility we are currently experiencing is that we need those folks if we are ever going to move past this divide.

Why? Because they are often in relationships that matter to us. Beyond that, we need to learn to talk to those with whom we disagree as the issues we face become even larger. And they vote.

Toward that end, here are ten ways to show respect as you engage in a difficult conversation with someone. Choose those that best fit your situation.

1. **Stay positive**. Refrain from using *don't, won't, can't, shouldn't, never* ...

Also, watch your body language; curb that impulse to raise an eyebrow, smirk, or yawn.

2. **Use I statements.** Speaking from your own reality is more effective than presenting a "This is how it is" statement. Here's where knowing the difference between an opinion and a fact is vital.

For example, say you propose a "fact" such as, "Too many Americans have no health care," your conversation partner can easily reply, "No, they don't." And down you'll both go into the morass.

Instead, if you offer what is clearly your opinion, "I am concerned that too many Americans have no health care," then, "No, you aren't" isn't a feasible response. How can they possibly argue with your opinion?

To help present your view of the future you desire, use sentences that begin with

*I'm concerned that . . .*

*I'm curious about . . .*

*I don't understand how . . .*

3. **Identify areas of agreement** as often as you can and name them. Can you agree on a future you both want

to see? What's your goal, your vision of the world you want to live in, you want your children to live in? I imagine we all want our children to grow up healthy, successful (however we define it), and at peace. What else can you agree on?

4. **Ask open ended questions** as opposed to ones that can be answered with a simple "yes" or "no."

*What do you suggest?*

*What do you think about ___?*

*What leads you to that conclusion?*

*What would you like to accomplish?*

*What is the most important thing to you?*

5. **Preface your distinctly different opinion with** some version of "I hear you. And I feel differently."

*I hear you saying . . . Here's how I see it . . .*

6. **Soften your response before you let it land.** Try these:

*It probably won't surprise you that I see this differently.*

*This one hits very close to home for me; I have strong feelings about it.*

7. **Stay focused on one issue at a time.** It's easy to tumble down the proverbial rabbit hole by jumping from topic to topic. If you see that happening, try,

*Can we stay with _____ for now?*

Or, simply restate your position, (like a mantra): *I think . . . Or I believe . . .*

8. **Agree to disagree.** In the end, it may be necessary to end the conversation without a new understanding of each other. That happens. Here's a suggestion if that should be your decision.

*We both have strong feelings about this. I don't think this is working right now.*

For other suggestions, review Chapter 3, A is for Assess, and pause and think.

9. **Consider the possibility that you could be wrong.** Hold that possibility in your heart and model it for your partner. Think of your belief as just that, a belief you hold (however tightly or loosely), rather than absolute truth. Let go of your need to be right. And recognize that what is accepted as fact today may change in the

53

future as new information, new evidence comes to light.

Keep this quote from American humorist Mark Twain in mind:

*It ain't what you don't know that gets you into trouble. It's what you know for sure that just ain't so.* Mark Twain

10. **Realize there are no winners or losers** in this conversation. You want to come out of it together, both better informed, ready and able to work together toward the common good. Together, you will try to solve a mystery.

**Your question before moving ahead:**

- What is your biggest challenge in finding and showing respect?

## A Resource for Chapter 6

David M. Abshire. *The Grace and Power of Civility: Commitment and Tolerance in the American Experience.* The Fetzer Institute's Essays on Deepening the American Experience

# 7

# O is for Observation

There are three things to observe: your partner, yourself, and the conversation. We'll take them one at a time.

## Observe your conversation partner.

When we talk about having a civil conversation with someone around a difficult topic, we're also talking about having the opportunity to make a connection with another human being. We are, after all, social animals; feeling connected helps that oxytocin to flow.

How do you think it is for them to be in this conversation with you? How do you know they are paying attention to you? What are the signs?

Here's what I noticed during a few recent conversations with unsuspecting family and friends over our caffeine-of-choice.

I felt heard when:

- They leaned forward, as though to catch every word.
- They asked follow up questions, seeking additional information.
- They asked clarifying questions.
- They paraphrased occasionally to make sure they understood me correctly.
- They looked directly at me without staring. Eye contact was easy and comfortable.

So much of life is simply paying attention. Start doing that with your everyday conversations. Think of it as practice.

## Observe yourself.

Are you staying respectful of the conversation? Are you being respectful of your partner? Do you know what you are feeling? Calm, compassionate, and connected? Or agitated, anxious, or angry?

If you aren't sure, take a minute, sit quietly and comfortably and follow your breath. Notice where your body expands on your inhale. Are your shoulders going up, or your chest rising? Or is your belly expanding?

If you can take what we call a "belly breath" — breathing so your belly actually moves out on your inhale — there's interesting new evidence that indicates that this simple act alone triggers the vagus nerve and activates the relaxation response of your parasympathetic nervous system. In lay terms: belly breathes help you relax. Try a few.

Now, begin to notice the sensations in your body: aches, tingling, tightness, numbness. Is something itchy? Scratch it. If it aches, rub it. Whatever the sensation is, once you've identified it, try to state it clearly.

*When you said that, I felt my stomach lurch for a moment. Isn't that interesting?*

*I'm feeling afraid right now and need to take a break. Shall we continue next week?*

*My stomach is in knots. I just don't feel safe. Good-bye.*

*I'm getting rather teary at the moment. I need a minute.*

Remember to pause and think, from Chapter 3: A is for Assess.

Whatever you notice as you observe yourself, give yourself the gift of time to process what you learn. Sometimes talking with an objective third person can be helpful.

## Observe the conversation.

How's it going? Does the conversation feel sincere? Authentic? Have you both let go of the need to be right? Are you both still curious?

Difficult conversations have a way of escalating in emotional intensity. Escalators include "you" statements (finger pointing, blaming, accusing) and certain types of body language like lowering or narrowing your eyebrows (another way of passing judgment), exchanging "a look" with a third party, or condescendingly patting the other.

There are many ways to de-escalate an emotionally intense conversation. Of course, speaking from your own reality by using "I" statements is a classic de-escalator. Likewise, simply pausing and naming what you are observing can be enough.

*I'm concerned things are getting more heated than I'm comfortable with; how about you? Shall we take a short break?*

Thwarting ploys – diversions, deflections, digressions – and provocative statements are sometimes used (even unconsciously) and throw a difficult conversation off track. The simplest way to disarm them is by naming them. Here are nine suggestions:

*It seems like you are changing the subject.*

*It feels like you are just following a formula.*

*I'm feeling unnerved. This feels like stonewalling.*

*Are you blaming me here? Accusing me of . . . ?*

*I want to listen to your POV, but I can't do it when you are yelling at me.*

*I simply don't believe you. I'd like to check out the veracity of your last statement before we continue. Shall we meet again in a week?*

*I really dislike sarcasm; it doesn't serve our purpose here and it feels insincere. Could you rephrase?*

*When you sit in silence like that, I get confused. Are you still in this conversation or shall we end it?*

*I see this has you very upset. I don't want to lose sight of what we were talking about though. Shall we just wait a few minutes or would you like to reschedule?*

A note here on responding to tears: you really needn't do anything other than sit quietly and let the person know they are seen. If they need a Kleenex, give them the chance to ask.

**Be aware of the distinction between process and content.** You want to focus on the process, the nature of the interaction, the essence of what's happening. Often, we can get bogged down in content, cognitions, facts. Here are four examples to get you back on track.

*I think we're getting lost.*

*I'm lost.*

*I'm feeling confused. Could we summarize what each of us has said so far?*

*The energy has dropped. Is there something that's not being said?*

Engaging in a difficult conversation to good effect requires honesty, vulnerability, and a willingness to listen and reflect and change. As you've no doubt noticed, I believe these conversations take curiosity, compassion, and courage. All are necessary; none alone are sufficient. Keep in mind that conflict offers a pathway to a deeper understanding of ourselves, and an opportunity to experience a new intimacy in our life.

**Some questions for you before moving on:**

- How do you know you are being heard? How do you know you have heard correctly?

## Resources for Chapter 7

Christopher Bergland. *Diaphragmatic Breathing Exercises and Your Vagus Nerve.* Psychology Today. May 16, 2017.

It's Alright to Cry, sung by Rosie Greer on the *Free To Be, You and Me* album. Available on YouTube.

Charlotte Kasl. *If the Buddha Married:* Part Seven: Making Friends with Conflict. Penguin Books. 2001.

Charlotte Kasl. *A Home for the Heart: Creating Intimacy with Loved Ones, Neighbors, and Friends.* Harper Collins. 1997.

NOTES

# NOTES

# G is for Gratitude

*Gratitude is an emotion of connectedness,
which reminds us we are part of a larger universe with all living
things.*

Did you know that simply expressing gratitude is good for you? In fact, you don't even have to identify something to be grateful for; you need only seek it and there is a positive impact on your brain.

I've been a gratitude junkie for many years and have experienced its power to change how I approach problems, how I interpret them, and how I resolve them. And so, given that FROG needed a G, I've added this "attitude of gratitude." You'll see a link in the Resources List at the end of this chapter to Jennifer Hofmann's weekly Action List that includes her "thank you" suggestions. Seeing these each week has helped me stay in a state of gratitude during this difficult time.

In addition to those thank you notes I send, I remember **how grateful I am to live in a country where critical, divisive political disagreement is not only tolerated, it is protected.**

Closer to home, I recognize that when I discover someone who is able to hold a civil conversation with me about issues on which we disagree, I am fortunate, indeed. If someone close to you is willing to have that difficult conversation so you can both better understand each other, I hope you will thank them; it is a gift.

*Gratitude can lead to feelings of love, appreciation, generosity, and compassion, which further open our hearts and help rewire our brains to fire in more positive ways.*

Here are a few more of my current gratitudes.

**I'm grateful for the enormous uptick in political activism** I have seen. Not only are contributions up across a huge swath of organizations with a wide range of missions I support, I'm also meeting interesting new people whom I would not otherwise have met.

**I'm grateful to see an increase in a basic understanding of how our system works,** an understanding that can only lead to the steps needed to improve it. I'm thinking of the Electoral College, redistricting Congressional districts (AKA gerrymandering), the crazy-making rules that currently exist within the Congress, and the way in which money has tainted the political process.

There is much to be done to move our country forward and there now exists the energy and the will to accomplish much. **I have hope.** And for that I am also grateful.

**Our final question in this series:**

- What are you grateful for these days?

## Resources for Chapter 8

*Vanessa Loder. Forbes Magazine.* "How To Rewire Your Brain For Happiness." March 2015.

Dr. Melanie Greenberg in *Psychology Today*, "How Gratitude Leads to a Happier Life." 2015. The two quotes chosen for this chapter are hers from *Psychology Today*, "The Seven Best Gratitude Quotes." 2011.

*Rewiring the Brain for Happiness: The Neuroscience of Happiness* by Kevin Corcoran. 2015.

Robert Emmons and Michael McCullough. *Counting Blessings Versus Burdens: An Experimental Investigation of Gratitude and Subjective Well-Being in Daily Life.* 2003.

Emmons has a more recent book, *Thanks!: How Practicing Gratitude Can Make You Happier* that reports, "Scientifically speaking, regular grateful thinking can increase happiness by as much as 25 percent." Not just happiness, but better sleep and more energy (which are directly connected, it seems to me) can result in only three weeks of keeping a gratitude journal.

Jennifer Hofmann's weekly Action List on her "Americans of Conscience Checklist." Be sure to check it out.

*Gratitude Practice Explained.* Yale Center for Emotional Intelligence.

# NOTES

# CONCLUSION

We humans are social animals and when we are estranged from others, we suffer. Unresolved interpersonal conflicts leave a trail of physical problems in its wake: tense muscles that lead to aches and pain, anger that builds and settles just below the surface eager to erupt unannounced, fear that knots in the stomach. We have much to gain from addressing conflict in general, or resolving a disagreement in particular.

This is not to say we must all agree. Of course we won't. But, if you're not quite ready to celebrate difference, perhaps you can appreciate how it is the source of all creativity. Indeed, think of difference as the beginning of all learning. Then, consider a disagreement as a difference of opinion that creates an enlightening and stimulating mystery, which can be solved: together.

Difficult conversations grounded in curiosity, compassion, and courage are not for the faint of heart. The idea of disagreement, of difference, scares many. Beliefs about the salience of skin color, religion, education level, country of origin, and other differences are tearing our country apart, and our inability to address those disagreements is taking us further and further from each other, increasing the polarization that is greater than at any time since the Civil War. Perhaps even leading us to another one?

Civil conversations are hard to find these days. Someone says to us, "We have to talk," and we look for ways to run. But, if the idea of holding a difficult conversation for the purpose of healing our divided world seems too frightening or unrealistic at present, know that it has been done before.

I'm thinking of the negotiations in the early 1990s between the African National Congress (ANC) and South Africa's ruling National Party, initially in secret, which led to the end of apartheid and the release of Nelson Mandela and other political prisoners.

I'm thinking of Northern Ireland, and their seemingly endless internal wars between the Protestants and Catholics, the Loyalists and the Republicans.

I'm thinking of the 50+ years of drug wars in Columbia, and the way in which two warring factions came together: FARC and ELN (google it).

I'm thinking of our own Civil War and of Lincoln's call to find our "better angels." Three generations later, in the 1930s and 1940s when fascism threatened to land on our shores, deep disagreements over urban-rural tension, imports and exports, electrical expansion into rural area, and soil erosion led to a New Deal program that gave rise to USDA programs we still have. Do you know how? Urban politicians went to rural farms across the Midwest and listened to them.

When people are given the opportunity to be heard without judgment, magic happens. Given the ability to freely posit a confident opinion and the experience of being involved in an important conversation, I believe people will find each other again.

As we end, I'm aware that I'm ending with more questions than I had when I began in 2017. I've written down those that remain intriguing for me.

- What is the best setting for holding what Socrates called a dialectic? Do we want that "public dialogue to uncover truth" or one-to-one conversations?

- Who initiates a civil conversation, or who goes first?
- Do both sides need to agree to have this conversation first, or can one party be seduced to participate?
- How might we better balance our concern for self?
- How do we counter specific lies and address false statements?
- How can we use silence effectively, not as an escalator or thwarting ploy?
- What is the difference between civility and politeness?
- What is the impact of culture on conflict resolution?
- How might the methods of Non-Violent Communication overlap with this LEAPFROG model?

Perhaps you too have been left with more questions than answers. Send them to me via my website's CONTACT page at *janetgivens.com* and let's work together to bring civil discourse back into common use.

Would LEAPFROG work in your community as an interactive workshop? I'm interested in leading some. Contact me so we can talk further.

# NOTES

# RESOURCES

Links are live in the eBook version, and on the LEARN
MORE page on my website, *janetgivens.com*

**Want some practice? Here are seven sites designed to
do just that.**

**All Sides.com** offers media reports on a range of current
topics, but always choosing three sources, "Left, Center,
and Right." It's been somewhat fascinating to me to widen
my reading, though I will admit I often find their
categorization scheme challenging my biases.

**Better-Angels.org** is *"a bipartisan network of leaders and
organizations whose vision is to reunite America. Our method is to
improve our society's approaches to conflict. We seek an America
with less uninformed animosity between left and right, less separation
of upscale America from the rest of America, and fewer good reasons
for the governed to hold the governing in contempt. To work for these*

*changes, we bring people together from across the divides to rethink currently polarized issues, show why reducing polarization is an urgent priority, conduct citizen education and leadership training, and recommend policy reforms that will permit progress and compromise to be substituted for impasse and frustration."*

Their mission: *Better Angels is a citizens' organization uniting red and blue Americans in a working alliance to depolarize America. We try to understand the other side's point of view, even if we don't agree with it. We engage those we disagree with, looking for common ground and ways to work together. We support principles that bring us together rather than divide us*

They take their name from Abraham Lincoln, who, in 1861, said:

*We are not enemies, but friends. We must not be enemies. Though passion may have strained, it must not break our bonds of affection. The mystic chords of memory...will yet swell the chorus of the Union, when again touched, as surely they will be, by the better angels of our nature.*

**CNVC.org** is the website for the Center for Non-Violent Communication, a global nonprofit organization dedicated to sharing Nonviolent Communication (NVC) around the world. From their website:

*NVC is about connecting with ourselves and others from the heart. It's about seeing the humanity in all of us. It's about recognizing our commonalities and differences and finding ways to make life wonderful for all of us.*

**Greater Good in Action's Active listening website** is out of the University of California at Berkeley. The site offers a step-by-step summary of active listening and a quiz to assess your level of empathy.

**HiFromtheOtherSide.com** will match you with someone "from the other side." Here's how they introduce themselves on their website:

*Since the election, many of us talked about getting out of our echo chambers to talk to someone who supported another candidate. Not to convince, but to understand. ... Once we find a match, we'll shoot you two an email introducing you for a one-on-one conversation.*

When I signed up in early 2017, they asked "What did you want to be when you grew up?" and offered a chance to add anything else I'd like to say. You can include your zip code so they can match you up with someone close to you, if you'd rather do a face to face meet. I chose not to give my zip code as I'm looking to do this via email first. And as of this writing, I've not heard from them but their website now includes a "join the waitlist" button.

**LivingRoomConversations.org** is *"a simple way that anyone with an open mind can engage with their friends in a friendly yet meaningful conversation about topics we care about. These conversations increase understanding, reveal common ground and allow us to discuss possible solutions. No fancy event or skilled facilitator is needed."*

This site works a bit differently than *Hi From the Other Side* in that "two friends of different perspectives" begin by inviting two more friends and the six gather together to go over an agreed upon topic (listed on the website), following their list of suggested opening questions.

**MoreInCommon.com** is an international initiative, set up in 2017 to build communities and societies that are stronger, more united and more resilient to the increasing threats of polarization and social division.

**RC.org** is the website for Re-evaluation Counseling, a movement in interpersonal relationships that's been growing since 1950. From their website:

*Re-evaluation Counseling is a process for freeing humans and society as a whole from distress patterns so that we may resume fully intelligent functioning. Re-evaluation Counseling is practiced in pairs, by people listening to each other and assisting each other to release painful emotions.*

## ADDITIONAL BOOKS I've read since settling on the LEAPFROG acronym

Mahzarin R. Banaji and Anthony G. Greenwald. *Blindspot: Hidden Biases of Good People.* Bantam. 2016.

Victor Frankl. *Man's Search for Meaning.* Beacon Press. 1946.

Jonathan Haidt has a nice piece about values of liberals and conservatives on the *Psychology Today* blog.

Steven Hawkins et al. *Hidden Tribes: A Study of America's Political Landscape.* 2018.

Jay Heinrichs. *Thank you for Arguing: What Aristotle, Lincoln, and Homer Simpson Can Teach Us About the Art of Persuasion.* 3rd. Edition. Three Rivers. Press. 2017.

George Lakoff, *Moral Politics: How Liberals and Conservatives Think.* U of Chicago Press.

Lillianna Mason. *Uncivil Agreement: How Politics Became Our Identity.* University of Chicago Press. 2018.

Parker Palmer. *Healing the Heart of Democracy: The Courage to Create a Politics Worthy of the Human Spirit.* Jossey-Bass. 2011

Steve Pinker. *Enlightenment Now: The Case for Reason, Science, Humanism, and Progress.* Viking Penguin Random House. 2018.

Carl Sagan. *The Demon-Haunted World: Science as a Candle in the Dark.* Ballantine Books. 1995.

Timothy Shafffer et al. *A Crisis of Civility?: Political Discourse and Its Discontents.* Routledge. 2019.

John Welwood. *Toward a Psychology of Awakening.* U of Chicago Press. 2000

# ABOUT THE AUTHOR

Janet Givens is a sociologist and Gestalt psychotherapist in the Green Mountains of Vermont. She also spent four years in a political science PhD program eager to better understand the history and the modern-day workings of her American government.

Born in northern New Jersey at the start of the baby boomer generation, she has both a BS (NYU) and an MA (Kent State, OH) in sociology and worked in non-profit development for 25 years. Her second career as a Philadelphia-based Gestalt psychotherapist went on hold in 2004 when she began her Peace Corps journey, the focus of her first memoir, *At Home on the Kazakh Steppe*.

Her first book, a textbook entitled *Stuttering* (Pro-Ed, Publisher), co-authored with C. W. Starkweather (now her husband), was the first textbook designed for people who stutter and the clinicians who treat them to read together. It was included in *Choice* Magazine's "Best Textbooks of 1997," a first in the speech pathology field.

Her second book, *At Home on the Kazakh Steppe: A Peace Corps Memoir*, won the Moritz Thomsen Peace Corps Experience Award for 2015, presented annually for "the best description of life in the Peace Corps."

She shares her life with Woody (C.W.) Starkweather and together they sing with the local hospice choir, host through AirBnB, and steward their thirty acres.

In addition to her private practice, Janet enjoys being "Grandma Janet" to five young Buckeyes and "alpha mom" to Sasha, her white shepherd. Reach her at *janetgivens.com*

# NOTES

# NOTES

# NOTES

# NOTES

Made in the USA
Middletown, DE
21 November 2019

79140031R00057